Living With...
Anxiety and Depression

Nancy Dickmann

Consultant: Marjorie Hogan, MD

BROWN BEAR BOOKS

Published by Brown Bear Books Ltd
4877 N. Circulo Bujia
Tucson, AZ 85718
USA

and

Studio G14, Regent Studios,
1 Thane Villas, London N7 7PH, UK

© 2023 Brown Bear Books Ltd

ISBN 978-1-78121-803-7 (library bound)
ISBN 978-1-78121-809-9 (paperback)

Library of Congress Cataloging-in-Publication Data available on request

Text: Nancy Dickmann
Consultant: Marjorie Hogan, MD, Professor of Pediatrics, University of Minnesota, Retired staff pediatrician, Hennepin Healthcare
Design Manager: Keith Davis
Children's Publisher: Anne O'Daly

Manufactured in the United States of America

CPSIA compliance information: Batch#AG/5651

Picture Credits
The photographs in this book are used by permission and through the courtesy of:

Front Cover: iStock: Iren Geo;
Interior: iStock: aquaArts studio 20–21; Shutterstock: aodaod 12-13, BroCreative 6, Jacek Chabraszewski 10, GOLFX 22t, , 22Brian A Jackson 6–7, Damir Khabirov 18–19, Monkey Business Images 14, 16, 22b, mybox 18, NDAB Creativity 4, Sergey Novikov 4–5, Prostock-studio 16–17, racorn 8, SeventyFour 20, Syda Productions 14–15, Veja 12, Wavebreakmedia 10–11.

All other artwork and photography
© Brown Bear Books.

t-top, r-right, l-left, c-center, b-bottom

Brown Bear Books has made every attempt to contact the copyright holder. If you have any information about omissions please contact: licensing@brownbearbooks.co.uk

Websites
The website addresses in this book were valid at the time of going to press. However, it is possible that contents or addresses may change following publication of this book. No responsibility for any such changes can be accepted by the author or the publisher. Readers should be supervised when they access the Internet.

Words in **bold** appear in the Words to Know on page 23.

Contents

Mental Health

Your body is an amazing machine. It can run, sing, and create! It works best when you keep it healthy. Staying active helps your body. So do eating well and getting enough sleep.

Your body can get sick or injured. Doctors are there to help.

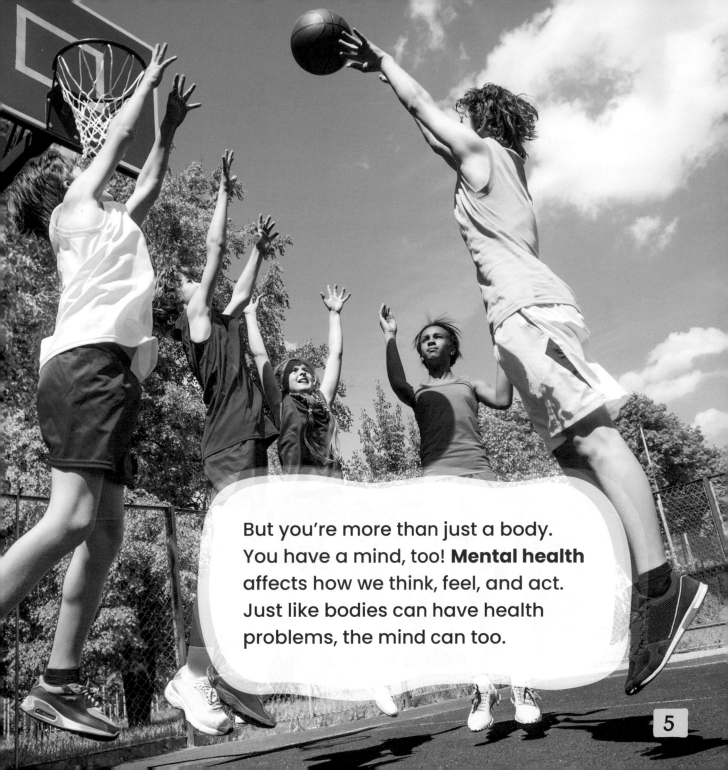

But you're more than just a body. You have a mind, too! **Mental health** affects how we think, feel, and act. Just like bodies can have health problems, the mind can too.

What Is Anxiety?

Some people don't like performing on stage. Others are nervous about meeting new people. Some people have fears about flying. Feeling worried is called anxiety.

Life is full of new experiences. Some of them can make you anxious.

Being anxious can make it hard to sleep. It might keep you from eating. It can give you a tummy ache. You might feel tense. You might find that you're always worrying.

As a toddler, Scott didn't like being separated from his parents. Later he had fears about throwing up. He was also scared of heights and flying. Scott was treated for anxiety.

What Is Depression?

Our moods and **emotions** are always changing. Sometimes you feel happy. Sometimes you feel sad. Sometimes you just feel a bit blah. But a person with depression feels sad and hopeless a lot.

You might feel sad if your team loses a big match.

A person with depression might:

- Feel sad
- Act grumpy or irritable
- Feel tired a lot
- Have trouble sleeping
- Avoid talking to friends and family
- Have trouble making decisions
- Lose weight or gain weight
- Feel like nothing matters
- Think about harming themselves
- Lose interest in things they used to enjoy

When It's a Problem

We all get worried sometimes. We all have times when we feel down. But anxiety and depression are more than that. The feelings don't go away. They make everyday life harder.

Exercise can boost your mood.
It releases special chemicals.
They make your brain feel happy.

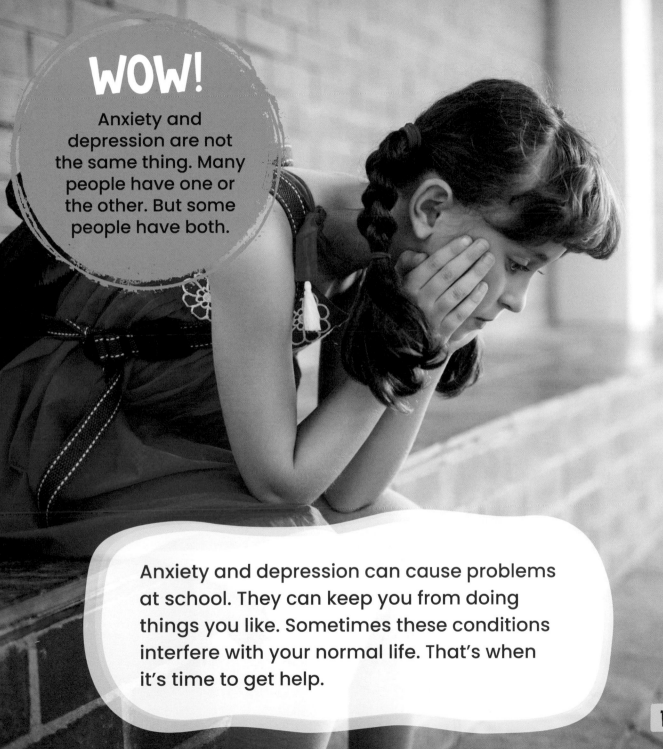

Anxiety and depression can cause problems at school. They can keep you from doing things you like. Sometimes these conditions interfere with your normal life. That's when it's time to get help.

You're Not Alone

Anxiety is a mental health problem. So is depression. They can make you feel lonely. You might feel like no one understands. But both are common problems. Anyone can have them.

Depression makes you hurt on the inside. Friends can't always tell you're hurting.

Some people know they have anxiety or depression. Others just know that something is wrong. Both problems can run in families. Parents and their children might both have them.

Nearly **1** in **10** children has anxiety.

About **1** in **23** have depression.

Causes

There are many causes for anxiety and depression. Some are things that happen to you. Bad experiences can make you feel worried or sad. But they are not your fault.

Some children get bullied at school. It can lead to anxiety or depression.

Do your parents argue? Does your family have money worries? Has someone you love died? These are all possible causes. Change can have an effect too. Moving to a new school or town is stressful.

WOW!

Climate change is a big problem. It makes many children anxious. Climate change affects everyone. But they feel helpless to stop it.

Getting Help

If you're having problems, talk to someone. Don't bottle things up. Sharing your problems can make them feel smaller. Go to an adult you trust. Don't be afraid to ask for help.

People with anxiety often avoid gatherings. They worry about being judged.

There is no blood test for anxiety or depression. A doctor will ask about your feelings. They will ask how they affect your life. You may need to see a mental health specialist.

Kayla stopped hanging out with her friends. She didn't like being around other people any more. Her family could tell something was wrong. They got help for her.

Medicines

There are pills for depression. Some also work on anxiety. Adults often take them. Sometimes children do too. The medicine acts on the brain. It changes the levels of some chemicals.

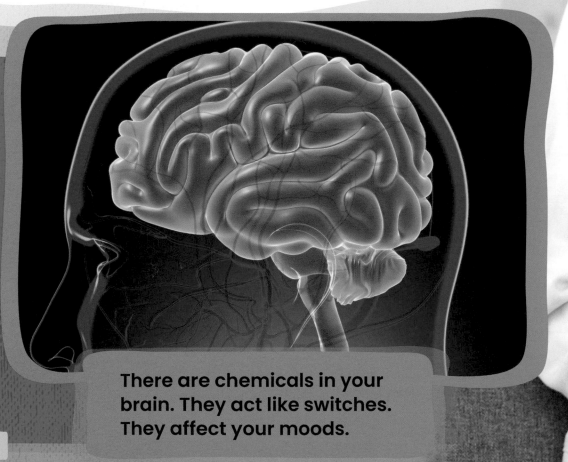

There are chemicals in your brain. They act like switches. They affect your moods.

These pills are not for everyone. They have **side effects**. They might make you feel sick or sleepy. Medicine won't make the illness go away. But it makes the **symptoms** easier to deal with.

Therapy

Pills are not the only solution. Talking can help. This is called **therapy**. Someone will listen and help. They might ask lots of questions. They want to understand your feelings.

Therapy can be one-to-one. It can also be done as a group.

Therapy will give you ways to manage your emotions. You'll get tips on coping with **stress**. Many people's symptoms improve.

Activity

People with anxiety often worry about the future. They think about bad things in the past. Mindfulness is a way to help. It's about focusing on the present.

Sit quietly and breathe deeply. Notice your breaths. Feel your chest rise and fall. Focus on the moment. How do you feel?

At your next meal, slow down. Focus on the food. How does it smell? How does it taste? Enjoy the flavors as you eat.

Words to Know

climate change the gradual warming of Earth's temperature, which causes weather disruption

emotions feelings such as joy, anger, or fear

mental health a person's condition in terms of their emotional well-being

side effects effects of a medicine that are not what it was designed to do

stress a feeling of emotional strain, as though everything is too hard

symptoms the outward signs of an illness, such as a fever, rash, or feeling

therapy a treatment with a person who is trained to listen and help deal with problems

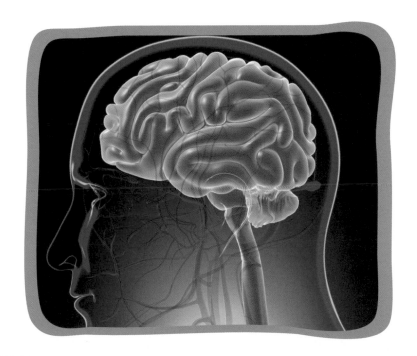

Find out More

Websites

bbcgoodfood.com/howto/
guide/10-mindfulness-exercises-
kids

dkfindout.com/us/human-body/
brain-and-nerves/brain/

kidshealth.org/en/kids/going-to-
therapist.html#catemotion

Books

Sometimes I Feel Sad
Jaclyn Jaycox, Capstone 2021

Worried (Everybody Feels...)
Moira Harvey, Quarto Publishing,
2020

**Your Brain Is Amazing:
How the Human Mind Works**
Esperanza Habinger, Orca Book
Publishers, 2023

Index